MW00513757

Copycat low-budget
Cookbook for beginners

Learn how to recreate and combine these 50 fast and tasty
recipes in the comfort of your kitchen.

William Oliver Thomas & Ernest D.W

© Copyright 2020 by

William Oliver Thomas & Ernest D.W

- All rights reserved.

The following Book is reproduced below with the goal of providing information that is as accurate and reliable as possible. Regardless, purchasing this Book can be seen as consent to the fact that both the publisher and the author of this book are in no way experts on the topics discussed within and that any recommendations or suggestions that are made herein are for entertainment purposes only. Professionals should be consulted as needed prior to undertaking any of the action endorsed herein. This declaration is deemed fair and valid by both the American Bar Association and the Committee of Publishers Association and is legally binding throughout the United States.

Furthermore, the transmission, duplication, or reproduction of any of the following work including specific information will be considered an illegal act irrespective of if it is done electronically or in print. This extends to creating a secondary or tertiary copy of the work or a recorded copy and is only allowed with the express written consent from the Publisher. All additional right reserved.

The information in the following pages is broadly considered a truthful and accurate account of facts and as such, any inattention, use, or misuse of the information in question by the reader will render any resulting actions solely under their purview. There are no scenarios in which the publisher or the original author of this work can be in any fashion deemed liable for any hardship or damages that may befall them after undertaking information described herein.

Additionally, the information in the following pages is intended only for informational purposes and should thus be thought of as universal. As befitting its nature, it is presented without assurance regarding its prolonged validity or interim quality. Trademarks that are mentioned are done without written consent and can in no way be considered an endorsement from the trademark holder.

Table of Content

Introduction

Dear Reader,

My name is William Oliver Thomas. I am an experienced chef with a passion for good food. With this book, I want to show you that you don't need a spell to prepare nutritious and delicious meals that taste just like those of famous restaurants.

In the coming chapters, we will first talk about the benefits of cooking at home. We will then move on to some practical tips for beginners on the proper distribution of meals, to digest well, and avoid gaining weight.

If we think, we know that a great start to the day does not require much. A healthy and abundant breakfast helps to start the day with vigor and the right amount of energy needed to deal with fatigue and stress.

For lunch, you could start the meal with a tasty soup or a light appetizer as the main course, then move on to a second course enriched by a crispy salad on the side, and don't forget the dessert that will help you stay in a good mood.

In this book, you'll find many recipes divided into different categories to enrich your dishes and enjoy every meal as a moment of full enjoyment! You'll be able to combine them with other recipes you've received from friends and family or with recipes you may have already tried in other restaurants.

Imagine hearing the sound of water boiling in the background as you chop fresh, crisp vegetables. Smell the intense aroma of spices and herbs as you stir sauces and dressings. Imagine the joy of your guests as they prepare for a delicious meal you are cooking for them.

Imagine the explosion of your taste buds as you enjoy the final flavor of your creations, accentuated by the satisfaction of having cooked and created everything yourself.

PS.

When I first learned to cook, I would randomly jot down the changes I made to the ingredients next to the dishes. I fold the corners of the pages to find my favorite recipes faster. My cookbooks were not pretty to look that. While writing this book, I decided to include a space for notes next to each recipe. You'll find a tab at the end of the book where you can note which page your favorite recipes are on.

Benefits of Cooking at Home

Meals in the restaurant can contain several unhealthy ingredients. There is also much more than what you lack when you feed on a take-outs. These are some explanations of why you should consider having your cooking dinner tonight!

A Nutrient-Dense Plate

If prepared food arrives from outside the home, you typically have limited knowledge about salt, sugar, and processed oils. For a fact, we also apply more to our meal when it is served to the table. You will say how much salt, sugar, and oil are being used to prepare meals at home.

Increased Fruit and Vegetable Intake

The typical western diet loses both the weight and durability of plant foods we need to preserve. Many People eat only two fresh fruit and vegetables a day, while at least five portions are required. Tons of premade food, like restaurant food goods, restrict fruit and vegetable parts. By supplying you with the convenience of cooking at home, you have complete control over your food. The message to note is that your attention will continue with the intake of more fruit and vegetables. Attach them to your cooking, snack them, or exchange them with your relatives on their way. Then take steps towards organic alternatives. It is always better to eat entire fruits and vegetables, whether or not organic, than processed foods.

Save Money and Use What You Have

Just because you haven't visited your local health food or food store this week doesn't mean you get stuck with taking in. Open your cupboard and fridge and see what you can make for a meal. It can be as easy as gluten-free rice, roasted tomatoes, carrots, frozen vegetables, and lemon juice. This simple meal is packed with fiber, protein, vitamins, and minerals. Best of all, in less than 30 minutes, it is delicious and can be prepared. You can save up your money in the long run and allows you sufficient food to share with or break the next day.

Sensible Snacking

Bringing premade snacks saves time, but everything goes back to what's in these products still. Don't worry, you can still have your guilty pleasures, but there is a way to make them more nutritious and often taste better. Swap your chips and dip the chopped vegetables into hummus. Create your snacks with bagged potato chips or carrots. Take a bowl and make your popcorn on top of your stove or in the popcorn machine. You can manage the amount of salt, sugar, and oil added.

Share Your Delicious Health

Once you make your recipes, you are so proud of your achievements. Furthermore, the food tastes amazing. Don't confuse me now–some of your inventive recipes won't taste the same thing, but friends and family will love your cuisine with constant practice and experimentation. You will see them enjoy the best nutritious food because of you and your faith in spreading health and love.

It Gives You a Chance to Reconnect

Having that chance to cook together helps you reconnect with your partner and your loved ones. Cooking also has other benefits. The American Psychological Association says that working together with new things—like learning a new recipe—can help maintain a relationship.

It's Proven to Be Healthier

Many researchers say that those who eat more often than not have a healthier diet overall. Such studies also show that in restaurants, menus, salt, saturated fat, total fat, and average calories are typically higher than in-house diets.
You have complete control over your food, whether you put fresh products together or shipped them straight to your door using a company like Plated. It can make a difference in your overall health.

It's Easier to Watch Your Calories

The average fast-food order is between 1,100 and 1,200 calories in total—nearly all the highly recommended daily calorie intake is 1,600 to 2,400 calories by a woman and almost two thirds (2,000 to 3,000 calories) a man daily. So, think again if you felt the independent restaurants so smaller chains would do well. Such products suck up an average of 1.327 calories per meal of additional calories.

Adult BMI Calculation Formula

$$BMI = \frac{\text{(your weight in pounds)} \times 703}{\text{(your height in inches)}^2}$$

FOR EXAMPLE:

If you weigh **120 pounds** and are **5 ft. 3in** (63in.) tall:

$$BMI = \frac{120 \times 703}{63^2} = \frac{84,360}{3,969} = \mathbf{21.3}$$

This is well within the healthy weight range

Creating your food ensures you can guarantee that the portion sizes and calories are where you want them. Recipes also come with nutritional information and tips for sizing, which ease this.

Body Mass Index Interpretation

BMI < 18.5: Below normal weight
BMI >= 18.5 and < 25: Normal weight
BMI >= 25 and < 30: Overweight
BMI >= 30 and < 35: Class I Obesity
BMI >= 35 and < 40: Class II Obesity
BMI >= 40: Class III Obesity

It's a Time Saver

Part of shopping is to wait for food to come or travel to get it. It may take much more time, depending on where you live, what time you order, and whether or not the delivery person is good at directions!
It doesn't have to take much time to cook at home if you don't want it. You remove the need to search for ingredients or foodstuffs by using a service like Plated. Everything you need is at your house, in the exact amount that you use.

It can be a money saver, too

In the long run, home-cooked food will save you money. A collection of basic ingredients also arrive at a lower price than a single dish. You can also consume more of a meal at home than if you buy a take-out or rest to work the next day. After a few weeks, you will see big savings starting to add up

It's Personalized

Cooking at home gives you the chance to enjoy the food you want, how you like it. For starters, with Plated, if you want your meat more well-done or less sweet, the formula includes suggested changes.

Cutting Costs

Nobody has to remind you that it's pricey to eat out. The disparity between a local restaurant sandwich and a kitchen sandwich is more than a feeling. The purchasing of packaged food in a restaurant typically costs far more than the buying of your
products. Cooking at home helps you get more for your money by raising the excess expenses of cooking and servicing restaurants. The more often you make your food, the more money you save.

Enjoying the Process

Once you come back home from a busy day, there is little more enjoyable than disconnecting from work emails, voicemails, unfinished assignments, or homework. Cooking at home presents you with a break from your routine and space for imagination. Rather than listen to noisy messages, you should put on the radio, collect spices, and reflect on the sizzle's odors on the stove or roast vegetables. It may stun you on how much you might like it when you make a daily habit of preparing food.

If your breakfast is great, lunch soup, or fresh tomato sauce for dinner, home cooking is a worthy investment. In return for your time and energy in preparation, you will benefit richly— from cost savings to fun with friends.

And the more you enjoy cooking in the kitchen, the more you get to make fantastic food!

Try Plated

Ready to download and cook your smartphone? Plated is a kind of a meal kit delivery service that offers all the above and more positive features! Choose from a weekly menu of designed recipes and get all you need right at your door. Pre-portioned foods are of the highest quality only and contain fresh, seasonal, organically, and sustainable seafood items and hormone-free meat.

Recipes vary from meals that require just 30 minutes to prepare, which is as demanding as its rewards. Where people find dinner a delight to consume and cook.

Practical Advice for Beginners on the Correct Distribution of Meals During the Day, to Digest Well and Avoid Gaining Weight

Shifting to a healthy lifestyle seems to be intimidating. Being committed to your preferred diet, slowly and reasonably, will provide you lifelong changes and optimum health.

Start by selecting what seems doable to you. Follow your instincts when something piques your interest. You are the best at knowing what's right for you and what you will or will not eat or drink.

Be willing to trying something new because you will have to do something different, on purpose, if you want a different result. Don't worry about what you might give up. You don't have to decide to give up anything right now. Keep it easy. Once you go through the benefits of feeling better, having more energy, and looking better, it will be easier to embrace and maintain a healthy eating lifestyle.

The effortless mistake we've made by just only eating our food makes it a significant difference. It is vital to think that when it comes to our meals, timing is the key.

As for your breakfast, eating within 30 minutes of waking up is essential. 7 in the morning is the best time to have breakfast. Make sure to have your meal no later than 10 a.m. and always have protein in your breakfast.

Lastly, at 7 p.m., dinner is the perfect time to have your meal. It would be perfect for you to keep a 3 hours gap between dinner and bedtime. Have your meal before 10 p.m. because eating dinner close to bedtime might affect your good night's sleep.

One way to adapt a healthy eating lifestyle is to add vegetables and fruit to what you already eat gradually.
• At breakfast, include bananas, blueberries, blackberries, strawberries, or raspberries. Add spinach, onions, or bell peppers to eggs or egg whites.
• At lunch, have a cup of vegetable soup or a salad with your meal.
• At dinner, include an extra serving or two of vegetables.

In between meals, try having a piece of fruit such as orange, peach, apple or pear, or vegetables like celery, cucumber, carrots, tomatoes, or bell pepper. Meal dynamics is a way of saying that it's not just what you eat and when you eat that matters; how you eat matters, too! There are few variables in how one eats.

Your sequence: Main dish, salads, then dessert? How about having dessert first to guarantee that there is still room, instead of filling it all up? It is vital to deliberate on how customs lead us and to know whether it all makes sense. If you learn to yourself you want to have dessert, why not eat it first so you'll have time to relish it instead of stuffing it in when you're full?

Pace and duration: Are the meal more like a tweet or an essay? Is it more evocative of a furious choreography or ballroom dance? How long does it take to consume the meal?

Timing: If you have an AC eating schedule on your meals, do you eat your meal at the start of the eating window? Or at the end? Or do you nibble snack portion of foods through the window? Does it change anything if you eat carbohydrates first or last?

It can also be introduced that eating too heavy and too late promotes bad dreams, and the body focuses only on digestion and not on the regenerative processes of the body such as: skin renewal, treatment of infections and injuries of the body, hormones of satiety are not produced, the same as when you consume too much alcohol before going to bed.

Fast food may be adding to surplus fat in ways that go beyond being loaded with calories and engineered to have a compelling, appetite-stimulating taste and mouthfeel. Fast food is fast in another way: not only is it available quickly, but people tend to eat it and digest it promptly with complete absorption. The suitability of snacks such as burgers, smoothies, and fries help you achieve your calorie intake worth for a day in those 10 minutes of eating them. With all of those calories flowing down to your throat, you won't be able to measure your calorie intake from the first bite of your meal. You just paid for the meal, so you eat every edge to get the maximum value. It may not be ideal, because those extra bites expand your stomach, so it will allow you to eat more food later on to have that same feeling of fullness. Stomach stretch is a viral sensation that helps you know when you've had enough; it prevents you from spraining your stomach by savoring those extra bites. You get your superior value by having those different bites later, if not necessary, getting rid of those excess calories is still better than stuffing it into your body. Be mindful of ordering meals to avoid left-overs.

To use meal dynamics as a tool, you:

1. Eat low-calorie, high-volume foods first: Soups and salads are great for this for reasons mentioned in the "Meal Composition" section. Besides soups and salads, you can snack on pickles, cucumbers, celery, carrots, grape tomatoes, and other low-calorie foods with high water content instead of concentrated calorie juice, nuts, chips, or rapidly digested foods. Remember the Super-BCPs? (Sugars, pasta, rice, bread, cereal, and potatoes).

2. Nutrition experts say that you should focus on food by consciously sniffing and tasting so that your body can record the act of eating.

Take your time! Meals are not a pit stop where every second you reduce your eating time is an advantage for the daily rush.

Enjoy the aromas and the company of other people...

And if you have to eat alone, don't get tangled up in other activities at the same time. Do not chew or swallow hastily.
Bon appetite! If you take less than half an hour to eat, don't let your stomach and brain record everything you've eaten.
The dynamic of eating is to listen to your body and feel the natural feeling of satiety.
Even if you eat fast food, you can correct your appetite by eating it slowly.

Breakfast Recipes

Delicious Potato Doughnuts

Preparation Time: 20 minutes
Cooking Time: 40 minutes.
Servings: 4

Ingredients:

- 2 mugs warm mashed potatoes (with included milk and butter).
- 2-1/2 cups sweets.
- 2 mugs buttermilk.
- 2 big eggs, softly beaten.
- 2 tbsps. Butter, melted.
- 2 teaspoons baking soda.
- 2 teaspoons cooking particle.
- 1 teaspoon sodium.
- 1 tsp ground nutmeg.
- 6-1/2 to 7 mugs all-round flour.
- Oil for deep-fat frying.

Fast Fudge Frosting:

- 3-3/4 cups confectioners' glucose.
- 1/2 cup baking chocolate.
- 1/4 tsp sodium.
- 1/3 cup boiling water.
- 1/3 cup butter, liquefied.
- 1 tsp vanilla extract.

Directions:

1. In a big bowl, mix the potatoes, glucose, buttermilk, and eggs. Mix in the butter, baking soda, cooking powder, sodium, nutmeg, and enough of the flour to establish a smooth dough.

2. Turn onto a lightly floured surface; tap bent on 3/4-in. fullness. Reduce with a 2-1/2- in. floured doughnut cutter machine.
3. In an electricity frying pan, warm 1 in. of oil to 375 °. Pan fry the doughnuts for 2 mins on each edge or even until browned.
4. Place on towels made from paper for frosting, combine the confectioners' sweets, cocoa, and sodium in a big dish. Stir in the water, butter, and vanilla. Plunge leadings of hot pastries in the frosting.

Nutrition:

226 Calories, 15mg Cholesterol, 35g Carb

My notes:

Eggs Benedict with Homemade Hollandaise

Preparation Time: 30 minutes
Cooking Time: 10 minutes
Servings: 8

Ingredients:

- 4 big egg yolk sacs
- 2 tbsps. water
- 2 tablespoons lemon juice
- 3/4 cup butter, thawed
- Dash white colored pepper
- 8 big eggs
- 4 English buns, crack and cooked
- 8 pieces Canadian bacon, heated Paprika

Directions:

1. For the white sauce, whisk egg yolk packets, water, and lemon juice until blended in top of a double central heating boiler or even steel fantastic churning water, chef up until the mixture is thick enough to cover a steel spoon and temperature exceeds 160 °, mixing consistently.

2. Take off fire. Gradually drizzle excessively in soft melted oil, whisking continuously. Blend with chili pepper. Switch to a small bowl if need be. Place dish in a comfortable water bowl far larger than this.

3. Just keep dry, rousing occasionally, about 30 minutes till all set to serve. Spot 2-3 in. of water in a huge saucepan or even a frying pan with high sides. Offer a boil; readjust heat to sustain a gentle simmer. Crack 1 egg right into a small dish, having dish closed next to the water, slide the egg into the water.

4. Repeat with 3 additional eggs.

5. Chef, exposed, 2-4 moments, or whites are completely formed, and bags of yolk are not yet difficult to enlarge. Take eggs out of the water using a slotted spoon;

6. Repeat with 4 eggs in the process. Cover one-half of each muffin with a slice of bacon, a poached egg, and 2 teaspoons of sauce; sprinkle with paprika. Serve forthwith.

Nutrition:
345 Calories, 26g Fats, 15g Carbohydrate

My notes:

Buttermilk Pancakes

Preparation Time: 10 minutes
Cooking Time: 5 minutes
Servings: 2 dozen

Ingredients:
- 4 cups versatile flour.
- 1/4 cup sugar.
- 2 teaspoons cooking soda.
- 2 teaspoons salt.
- 1-1/2 teaspoons cooking grain.
- 4 large eggs, room temperature.
- 4 cups buttermilk.

Directions:
1. In a large bowl, combine the flour, sweets, cooking soft drink, salt, and cooking particle.
2. In an additional bowl, whisk the eggs and buttermilk until mixed; mix them into dry-out ingredients simply till dampened.
3. Pour batter by 1/4 cups onto a lightly buttered scorching griddle; turn when blisters form on top. Cook until the 2nd side is golden brown.
4. Freeze alternative: Freeze cooled down hot cakes between levels of waxed paper in a freezer container.

5. To make use of side hot cakes on an ungreased flat pan, cover with aluminum foil and reheat in a preheated 375 ° stove 6-10 moments.
6. Or place a stack of 3 hot cakes on a microwave-safe layer and microwave on high for 45-90 seconds or even up until warmed.

Nutrition:
270 Calories, 3g Fats, 48g Carb

My notes:

Ham and Swiss Omelet

My notes:

Preparation Time: 20 minutes
Cooking Time: 10 minutes
Servings: 1

Ingredients:

- 1 tablespoon butter
- 3 eggs
- 3 tbsps. water
- 1/8 teaspoon sodium
- 1/8 teaspoon pepper
- 1/2 cup cubed fully cooked ham
- 1/4 cup cut Swiss cheese

Directions:

1. In a little nonstick skillet, liquefy butter over medium-high temperature. Blend the eggs, pepper, water, and sodium. Add egg mixture to skillet (mixture must set quickly at edges).
2. As eggs prepared, press cooked sides toward the midpoint, allowing raw section circulation below.
3. When the eggs are established, place ham on one edge and sprinkle with cheese; fold the opposite side over the filling. Slide omelet onto a layer.

Nutrition:

530 Calories, 726mg Cholesterol, 4g Carb

Pecan Braid

Preparation Time: 30 minutes

Cooking Time: 25 minutes

Servings: 4

Ingredients:
- 1 package active dry yeast (¼ ounce)
- 3 beaten eggs, large
- 1 cup cold butter, cubed
- ½ cup sugar
- 5 cups all-purpose flour
- 1 cup warm water, divided (110 to 115 F)
- ½ teaspoon salt

For Filling:
- 1 cup packed brown sugar
- 1 cup butter, softened
- 1 tablespoon ground cinnamon
- 1 cup chopped pecans

For Glaze:
- ½ teaspoon vanilla extract
- 1 tablespoon butter, melted
- 1 ½ cups confectioners' sugar
- 1 to 2 tablespoons milk

Directions:
1. Dissolve yeast in ¼ cup of warm water in a large bowl. Add eggs and leftover water; mix well. Combine flour together with sugar & salt in a separate bowl. Cut in the butter until crumbly. Beat into yeast mixture (ensure that you don't knead). Cover & refrigerate overnight.

For filling:
2. Cream butter together with brown sugar in a small bowl. Stir in the cinnamon and pecans; set aside.

3. Turn the dough onto a lightly floured surface; evenly divide into four portions. Roll each into a 12x9" rectangle on a lightly greased baking sheet. Spread the filling lengthwise down the middle third of each rectangle.

4. One each long side, cut ¾" wide strips to the middle to within ½" of the filling. Beginning at one end, fold alternately strips at an angle across filling. Pinch ends to seal and tuck under. Cover & let rise for an hour in a warm place.

5. Bake until golden brown, for 18 to 20 minutes at 350 F. Before removing them from the pans to wire racks; let them slightly cool. Combine the entire glaze ingredients & drizzle the mixture on top of the cooled braids.

Nutrition:

836 Calories, 59g Fats, 36.9g Protein

My notes:

Wild Blueberry Muffin

Preparation Time: 10 minutes

Cooking Time: 1 hour and 5 minutes

Servings: 10

Ingredients:

For the Muffins:

- 1 ½ cup all-purpose flour
- 2 teaspoon baking powder
- ¾ cup granulated white sugar
- 1 large egg
- 2 teaspoon vanilla extract
- Old-fashioned buttermilk
- ⅓ cup vegetable oil
- 1 cup frozen wild blueberries
- ½ teaspoon salt

For the Topping:

- ⅓ cup raw sugar
- 4 tablespoon unsalted butter cold & cut into four pieces
- ⅓ cup all-purpose flour

Directions:

1. Line a jumbo muffin pan with 6-cup with paper liners and preheat your oven to 400 F in advance.
2. Combine coarse sugar together with cold butter and ⅓ cup flour in a small bowl. Mix the topping well using a pastry cutter until it's fine & crumbly. Store in a refrigerator until ready to use.
3. Now, whisk 1 ½ cups of flour together with baking powder, sugar & salt in a large bowl. Measure the oil in a 1-cup glass measuring cup & add the egg; whisk well. Pour in a little more than ⅓ cup of buttermilk until the liquid is approximately 8 fluid ounces. Add in the vanilla; whisk again.

4. Pour the wet mixture into the dry mixture; gently stir using a spatula or wooden spoon until just a few streaks of the flour remain. Add in the blueberries; gently mix until evenly distributed in the muffin batter.
5. Evenly divide the prepared batter among the muffin cups. Generously sprinkle the top of each muffin with the topping.
6. Bake the muffins on the center rack of your preheated oven until a toothpick comes out clean, for 28 to 30 minutes. Let completely cool. Store in an air-tight container for up to 2 days.

Nutrition:
867 Calories, 56g Fats, 40g Protein

My notes:

Energizing Smoothie & Milk Shake Recipes

Mega Mango Smoothie

Preparation Time: 5 minutes

Cooking Time: 0 minutes

Servings: 2

Ingredients:

- 1 cup frozen mangos
- 1 cup frozen strawberries
- ½ cup orange juice
- ½ cup pineapple juice
- 1 cup ice

Directions:

1. Blend all the ingredients until smooth consistency.

Nutrition:

590 Calories, 35g Fats, 8g Protein

My notes:

Orange-A-Peel Smoothie

Preparation Time: 10 minutes
Cooking Time: 0 minutes
Servings: 2

Ingredients:
- ½ banana, sliced
- 1 cup frozen strawberries
- 1 cup orange juice
- ½ cup vanilla nonfat frozen yogurt
- 1 cup ice

Directions:
1. Blend all the ingredients until smooth consistency.

Nutrition:
529 Calories, 34g Fats, 6g Protein

My notes:

Orange-C Booster Smoothie

Preparation Time: 10 minutes
Cooking Time: 0 minutes
Servings: 1

Ingredients:
- ½ banana, sliced
- ½ cup frozen peaches
- 1 cup orange juice
- 1 cup orange sherbet
- 1 cup ice
- Antioxidant Power Boost
- Immunity Boost

Directions:
1. Put all the ingredients and fill it to the max water line, then blend until smooth.

Nutrition:
550 Calories, 29g Fats, 4.9g Protein

My notes:

Orange Carrot Karma Smoothie

Preparation Time: 10 minutes
Cooking Time: 0 minutes
Servings: 2

Ingredients:
- ½ banana, sliced
- ½ cup frozen mangos
- 1 cup carrot juice
- 1 cup orange juice
- 1 cup ice

Directions:
1. Put all the ingredients and fill it to the max water line, then blend until smooth.

Nutrition:
603 Calories, 24g Fats, 5g Fiber

My notes:

Orange Dream Machine Smoothie

Preparation Time: 10 minutes
Cooking Time: 0 minutes
Servings: 2

Ingredients:

- ½ cup orange juice
- ½ cup soy milk
- 1 cup vanilla nonfat frozen yogurt
- 1 cup orange sherbet
- 1 cup ice
- Lemon Zest

Directions:

1. Put all the ingredients and fill it to the max water line, then blend until smooth.

Nutrition:

491 Calories, 29g Fats, 2g Fiber

My notes:

Peach Mango Smoothie

Preparation Time: 5 minutes

Cooking Time: 0 minutes

Servings: 2

Ingredients:
- 1 cup frozen mangos
- 1 cup frozen peaches
- ½ cup peach juice
- ½ cup soy milk
- 1 cup ice
- Balance Boost
- Lean Advantage Boost

Directions:
1. Put all the ingredients and fill it to the max water line, then blend until smooth.

Nutrition:
449 Calories, 28g Fats, 5g Fiber

My notes:

Peach Pleasure Smoothie

Preparation Time: 5 minutes

Cooking Time: 0 minutes

Servings: 1

Ingredients:

- ½ banana, sliced
- 1 cup frozen peaches
- 1 cup peach juice
- ½ cup orange sherbet
- 1 cup ice

Directions:

1. Put all the ingredients and fill it to the max water line, then blend until smooth.

Nutrition:

501 Calories, 31g Fats, 6g Fiber

My notes:

Peanut Butter Moo'd Smoothie

Preparation Time: 12 minutes
Cooking Time: 0 minutes
Servings: 2

Ingredients:

- ½ banana, sliced
- ½ cup peanut butter
- ½ cup chocolate milk
- 1 cup soy milk
- ½ cup vanilla nonfat frozen yogurt
- 1 cup ice

Directions:

1. Put all the ingredients and fill it to the max water line, then blend until smooth.

Nutrition:

489 Calories, 26g Fats, 3.9g Fiber

My notes:

Jamba Juice Pomegranate Paradise Smoothie

Preparation Time: 5 minutes

Cooking Time: 0 minutes

Servings: 1

Ingredients:

- ½ cup frozen mangos
- ½ cup frozen peaches
- 1 cup frozen strawberries
- 1 cup pomegranate juice
- 1 cup ice

Directions:

1. Put all the ingredients and fill it to the max water line, then blend until smooth.

Nutrition:

481 Calories, 23g Fats, 7g Protein

My notes:

Pomegranate Pick-Me-Up Smoothie

Preparation Time: 5 minutes
Cooking Time: 0 minutes
Servings: 2

Ingredients:

- ½ cup frozen blueberries
- ½ cup frozen strawberries
- ½ cup mixed berry juice
- ½ cup pomegranate juice
- 1 cup raspberry sherbet
- 1 cup ice

Directions:

1. Put all the ingredients and fill it to the max water line, then blend until smooth.

Nutrition:

501 Calories, 26g Fats, 4g Fiber

My notes:

Protein Berry Workout Smoothie

Preparation Time: 5 minutes
Cooking Time: 0 minutes
Servings: 2

Ingredients:
- ½ banana, sliced
- 1 cup frozen strawberries
- 1 cup soy milk
- 1 cup ice
- Whey Protein Boost

Directions:
1. Put all the ingredients and fill it to the max water line, then blend until smooth.

Nutrition:
440 Calories, 28g Fats, 6g Fiber

My notes:

Razzamatazz Smoothie

Preparation Time: 10 minutes
Cooking Time: 0 minutes
Servings: 2

Ingredients:

- ½ banana, sliced
- 1 cup strawberries
- 1 cup raspberry juice
- 1 cup orange sherbet
- 1 cup ice

Directions:

1. Put all the ingredients and fill it to the max water line, then blend until smooth.

Nutrition:

491 Calories, 29g Fats, 8g Fiber

My notes:

Sonic's Copycat Strawberry Shake

Preparation Time: 5 minutes

Cooking Time: 0 minutes

Servings: 2

Ingredients:

- 1½ cups vanilla ice cream
- ⅓ cup 2% milk
- 1 tablespoon strawberry preserves
- ½ cup frozen strawberries

Directions:

1. Blend all the ingredients until smooth. Pour into chilled glasses and serve.

Nutrition:

649 Calories, 35g Fats, 8g Protein

My notes:

Disney's Copycat Jelly Peanut Butter Milkshake

Preparation Time: 5 minutes
Cooking Time: 0 minutes
Servings: 2

Ingredients:

- 3 cups vanilla ice cream
- ¼ cup peanut butter
- 3–4 tablespoons grape jelly
- ¼–⅓ cup milk

Directions:

1. Combine the jelly and peanut butter in a bowl. Add the ice cream, jelly mix, and milk to a blender or food processor and blend to make a smooth mixture. Serve chilled.

Nutrition:

688 Calories, 33g Fats, 11g Protein

My notes:

In-N-Out Burger's Copycat Vanilla Shake

Preparation Time 10 minutes

Cooking Time: 0 minutes

Servings: 2

Ingredients:
- ½ cup whole milk
- 2 cups French vanilla ice cream
- 1 tablespoon Smucker's caramel topping

Directions:
1. Add the milk and ice cream to a blender or food processor. Blend for 30 seconds until the mixture is smooth. Add the caramel and blend again until mixed well.
2. Pour the mixture into a 12-ounce glass and serve chilled. Alternatively, place the blender in the freezer for 30 minutes and serve after stirring a bit if you like a thicker version.

Nutrition:
680 Calories, 37g Fats, 9g Protein

My notes:

Lunch and Dinner Recipes

Chicken-Fried Steak & Gravy Boat

Preparation Time: 30 minutes
Cooking Time: 20 minutes
Servings: 4

Ingredients:

- 1-1/4 mugs versatile flour, divided
- 2 big eggs
- 1-1/2 cups 2% milk, split
- 4 beef cube steaks (6 ozs each).
- 1-1/4 teaspoons salt, divided.
- 1 tsp pepper, broken down.
- Oil for panning fry.
- 1 cup water.

Directions:

1. Add 1 cup of flour in a shallow platter. Toss eggs and 1/2 cup milk in a separate small pot, until mixed.
2. Sprinkle steaks with 3/4 tsp each sodium and pepper. Dip in flour to coat each side; get away from excess.
3. Plunge in egg mixture, at that point once again in flour. Warm 1/4 in. In a large skillet of oil over warm substance.
4. Remove steaks; cook until golden brownish, and a thermostat reads on each side through 160 °, 4-6 mins.
5. Remove the towels from the pot; drain abstractly. Hold warm.

6. Remove about 2 tablespoons oil from pot. Stir in the staying 1/4 cup flour, 1/2 tsp salt, and 1/4 teaspoon pepper until smooth; chef and stir over medium heat up until golden brown, 3-4 moments.
7. Progressively whip in water and continue with the milk.
8. Offer a boil, stirring continuously; prepare and mix up until expanded, 1-2 mins. Serve with steaks.

Nutrition:
563 Calories, 28g Fats, 29g Carbohydrate

My notes:

Pei Wei's Sesame Chicken

Preparation Time: 20 minutes

Cooking Time: 15 minutes

Servings: 4 - 6

Ingredients:

Sauce:

- ½ cup soy sauce
- 2½ tablespoons hoisin sauce
- ½ cup sugar
- ¼ cup white vinegar
- 2½ tablespoons rice wine
- 2½ tablespoons chicken broth
- Pinch of white pepper
- 1¼ tablespoons orange zest

Breaded chicken:

- 2 pounds boneless skinless chicken breasts
- ¼ cup cornstarch
- ½ cup flour
- 1 egg
- 2 cups milk
- Pinch of white pepper
- Pinch of salt
- ¼ vegetable oil
- ½ red bell pepper, chunked
- ½ white onion, chunked
- 1 tablespoon Asian chili sauce
- ½ tablespoon ginger, minced
- ¼ cup scallions, white part only, cut into rings
- 1 tablespoon sesame oil
- 1 tablespoon cornstarch
- 1 tablespoon water
- Sesame seeds for garnish

Directions:

1. Prepare the sauce by whisking all the ingredients together in a small saucepan. Bring to a simmer, then remove from the heat and set aside. Whisk the eggs, milk, salt, and pepper together in a shallow dish.

2. Mix the ¼ cup of cornstarch and flour together in a separate shallow dish. Dredge the chicken pieces in the egg mixture and then in the cornstarch/flour mixture. Shake off any excess, then set aside. Heat the vegetable oil over medium-high heat in a deep skillet or saucepan.

3. When hot, drop the coated chicken into the oil and cook for about 2–4 minutes. Remove from oil and place on a paper-towel-lined plate to drain. Make a slurry out of the 1 tablespoon of cornstarch and water.

4. In a different large skillet or wok, heat 1 tablespoon of sesame oil until hot. Add the ginger and chili sauce and heat for about 10 seconds. Add the peppers and onions and cook for another 30 seconds. Stir in the chili sauce and ginger and the sauce you made earlier and bring to a boil. Once it boils, stir in the cornstarch slurry and cook until the sauce thickens.

5. When the sauce is thick, add the chicken and stir to coat. Serve with rice, and sprinkle with sesame seeds.

Nutrition:

691 Calories, 10g Fats, 31g Protein

My notes:

Eggplant Parmesan

Preparation Time: 2 hours 15 minutes

Cooking Time: 10 minutes

Servings: 2–4

Ingredients:

- 1 medium Italian eggplant, peeled and cut into ½-inch slices
- 2 teaspoons kosher salt
- ½ cup all-purpose flour
- 1 cup eggs, beaten
- 2 cups Italian breadcrumbs
- ½ cup vegetable oil
- ¾ cup marinara sauce
- ¼ cup basil-infused olive oil
- 3 tablespoons Parmesan cheese, grated, divided
- 4 ounces mozzarella cheese, grated
- ⅛ teaspoon kosher salt
- 5 ounces angel hair pasta, cooked
- ½ teaspoon parsley, chopped

Directions:

1. Preheat the oven to broil. Line a baking sheet with paper towels. Season both sides of the eggplant circles with salt and arrange them on the pan. Cover the eggplant with another sheet of paper towel and refrigerate for 2 hours.
2. Place the flour in one bowl, the eggs in another, and the breadcrumbs in a third bowl.
3. After 2 hours, remove the eggplant from the fridge and dry the slices with a fresh paper towel. One at a time, dip the slices in flour, then in the egg, and finally in the breadcrumbs. Set them aside.
4. Cook the oil in a large skillet over medium heat. Fry the eggplant for about 2 minutes on each side and set them on a plate lined with a paper towel.

5. Cook the marinara sauce in a small saucepan and the basil oil in another small pan.
6. Place a wire rack in a baking dish and transfer the cooked eggplant slices to the rack. Sprinkle on 2 tablespoons of the Parmesan cheese and the mozzarella, then put the pan under the broiler until the cheese melts.
7. Serve the cooked pasta topped with eggplant. Pour some marinara over the top. Drizzle basil oil and sprinkle with the remaining Parmesan cheese and parsley.

Nutrition:
230 Calories, 14g Fats, 17.1g Carbs, 8g Protein

My notes:

Lasagna Fritta

Preparation Time: 20 minutes
Cooking Time: 4 minutes
Servings: 14

Ingredients:
- ⅔ + ¼ cup milk (divided)
- 1 cup grated parmesan cheese, plus some more for serving
- ¾ cup feta cheese
- ¼ teaspoon white pepper
- 1 tablespoon butter
- 7 lasagna noodles
- 1 egg
- Breadcrumbs
- Oil for frying
- 2 tablespoons marinara sauce
- Alfredo sauce, for serving

Directions:
1. Place the butter, white pepper, ⅔ cup milk, parmesan, and feta cheese in a pot. Stir and boil. Make lasagna noodles as stated on the package.
2. Spread a thin layer of the cheese and milk mixture on each noodle. Fold into 2-inch pieces and place something heavy on top to keep them folded. Place in the freezer for at least 1 hour, then cut each noodle in half lengthwise.

3. In a small bowl, mix the ¼ cup milk and egg together. In another bowl, place breadcrumbs. Dip each piece into the egg wash, then the breadcrumbs. Fry the noodles at 350°F for 4 minutes.
4. Serve by spreading some alfredo sauce at the bottom of the plate, placing the lasagna on top, and then drizzling with marinara sauce. Sprinkle the grated parmesan cheese

Nutrition:

1070 Calories, 71g Fats, 73g Carbs, 35g Protein

My notes:

Fried Mozzarella

Preparation Time: 10 minutes
Cooking Time: 10 minutes
Servings: 4

Ingredients:
- 1-pound mozzarella or other cheese
- 2 eggs, beaten
- ¼ cup water
- 1½ cups Italian breadcrumbs
- ½ teaspoons garlic salt
- 1 teaspoon Italian seasoning
- ⅔ cup flour
- ⅓ cup cornstarch

Directions:
1. Slice thick cuts of the cheese. Blend together eggs and water for egg wash. Combine the breadcrumbs, garlic salt, and Italian seasoning. In another bowl, combine together flour and cornstarch.
2. Cook vegetable oil in a frying pan. Soak each piece of cheese into the flour, then egg wash, then breadcrumbs. Deep fry until golden brown. Set aside and drain on a paper towel. Serve with marinara sauce.

Nutrition:
100.8 Calories, 5.7g Fats, 7g Carbs, 4g Protein

My notes:

Gnocchi with Spicy Tomato and Wine Sauce

Preparation Time: 10 minutes
Cooking Time: 40 minutes
Servings: 4

Ingredients:
Sauce:

- 2 tablespoons extra virgin olive oil
- 6 fresh garlic cloves
- ½ teaspoon chili flakes
- 1 cup dry white wine
- 1 cup chicken broth
- 2 cans (14.5 ounces each) tomatoes
- ¼ cup fresh basil, chopped
- ¼ cup sweet creamy butter, cut into 1-inch cubes, chilled
- ½ cup parmesan cheese, freshly grated

Pasta:

- 1-pound gnocchi
- Salt, to taste
- Black pepper, freshly crushed, to taste

Directions:

1. Sauté the olive oil, garlic, and chili flakes in a cold pan over medium heat. When the garlic starts turning golden brown, stir in the wine and broth and let it simmer.

2. When the broth simmers down. Mix in the tomatoes and basil and then continue simmering for another 30 minutes. Once thickened, let it rest for 3 minutes.
3. After a few minutes, transfer the sauce in a blender, and stir in the butter and parmesan. Purée and set aside. Make the pasta by boiling the gnocchi in a large pot. When it is cooked, drain the pasta and blend the sauce. Serve.

Nutrition:
320.7 Calories, 22.5g Fats, 11.6g Carbs, 12.8g Protein

My notes:

Olive Garden's Cheese Ziti Al Forno

Preparation Time: 10 minutes
Cooking Time: 35 minutes
Servings: 8

Ingredients:
- 1 lb. Ziti
- 4 tbsp Butter
- 2 cloves Garlic
- 4 tbsp All-purpose flour
- 2 cups Half & Half
- A dash of Black pepper
- Kosher salt (as desired)
- 3 cups Marinara
- 1 cup - grated Parmesan - divided
- 2 cups Shredded mozzarella - divided

Other Shredded Cheese:
- ½ cup Fontina
- ½ cup Romano
- ½ cup Ricotta
- ½ cup Panko breadcrumbs

The garnish:
- Fresh Parsley

Directions:
1. Warm the oven to reach 375° Fahrenheit.
2. Spritz the casserole dish with cooking oil spray. Prepare a large pot of boiling - salted water to cook the ziti until al dente. Drain and set it to the side.
3. Mince the garlic. Shred/grate the cheese and chop the parsley.
4. Make the alfredo. Heat the skillet using the medium temperature setting to melt the butter. Toss in the garlic to sauté for about half a minute. Whisk in flour and simmer until the sauce is bubbling (1-2 min.).

5. Whisk in the Half-and-Half and simmer. Stir in ½ cup parmesan, pepper, and salt. Cook it until the sauce thickens (2-3 min.). Stir in the marinara, one cup of mozzarella, Romano, fontina, and ricotta. Fold in the pasta. Dump it into the casserole dish.

6. Combine ½ cup of the parmesan and the breadcrumbs. Sprinkle it over the top of the dish. Set the timer and bake until browned as desired and bubbly (30 min.). Garnish with parsley and serve.

Nutrition:
272 Calories, 20g Fats, 25g Carbs, 23g Protein

My notes:

Breaded Fried Okra

Preparation Time: 15 minutes

Cooking Time: 10 minutes

Servings: 4

Ingredients:
- 1-pound fresh okra, rinsed and dried
- 1 cup self-rising cornmeal
- ½ cup self-rising flour
- 1 teaspoon salt
- 1 cup vegetable oil (for frying)
- Salt and pepper to taste

Directions:
1. Cook the oil in a large skillet or deep fryer. Cut the okra into ½-inch pieces. Combine the cornmeal, flour, and salt in a large bowl. Drop the okra pieces into the bowl and toss to coat. Allow to rest for a few minutes while the oil heats up.
2. Using a slotted spoon, transfer the okra from the bowl into the hot oil. Cook for about 10 minutes or until the okra has turned a nice golden color.
3. Remove from oil and place on a plate lined with paper towels to drain. Season to taste with salt and pepper.

Nutrition:
18 Calories, 3.6g Carbs,
1g Protein, 2g Fiber

My notes:

Chicken Marsala

Preparation Time: 10 minutes

Cooking Time: 40 minutes

Servings: 4 - 6

Ingredients:

- 2 tablespoons olive oil
- 2 tablespoons butter
- 4 boneless skinless chicken breasts
- 1 ½ cups sliced mushrooms
- 1 small clove garlic, thinly sliced
- Flour for dredging
- Sea salt and freshly ground black pepper
- 1 ½ cups chicken stock
- 1 ½ cups Marsala wine
- 1 tablespoon lemon juice
- 1 teaspoon Dijon mustard

Directions:

Chicken scaloppini:

1. Pound out the chicken with a mallet or rolling pin to about ½ inch thick. In a large skillet, heat the olive oil and 1 tablespoon of the butter over medium-high heat. When the oil is hot, dredge the chicken in flour. Season with salt and pepper on both sides. Dredge only as many as will fit in the skillet. Don't overcrowd the pan.
2. Cook chicken in batches, about 1 to 2 minutes on each side or until cooked through. Remove from skillet, and place on an oven-proof platter. Keep warm in the oven, while the remaining chicken is cooking.

Marsala sauce:

3. In the same skillet, add 1 tablespoon of olive oil. On medium-high heat, sauté mushrooms and garlic until softened. Remove the mushrooms from the pan and set aside.

4. Add the chicken stock and loosen any remaining bits in the pan. On high heat, let reduce by half, about 6-8 minutes. Add Marsala wine and lemon juice and in the same manner reduce by half, about 6–8 minutes. Add the mushroom back in the saucepan, and stir in the Dijon mustard. Warm for 1 minute on medium-low heat. Remove from heat, stir in the remaining butter to make the sauce silkier.
5. To serve, pour the sauce over chicken, and serve immediately.

Nutrition:

487 Calories, 7.1g Carbs, 34g Protein

My notes:

Chicken Scampi

Preparation Time: 10 minutes
Cooking Time: 20 minutes
Servings: 4

Ingredients:
Pasta:

- ½ pound uncooked angel hair pasta
- ½ teaspoon canola or olive oil
- ¼ teaspoon salt

Chicken:

- 1-pound chicken tenderloins
- ½ cup all-purpose flour
- ¼ teaspoon salt
- ⅛ teaspoon ground pepper
- ¼ teaspoon Italian seasoning
- ⅓ cup whole milk
- 2 tablespoons oil
- Vegetables and sauce
- 2 tablespoons canola or olive oil
- ½ green pepper, sliced into thin strips
- ½ red pepper, sliced into thin strips
- ½ yellow pepper, sliced into thin strips
- ½ red onion, sliced thin
- 5 tablespoons unsalted butter
- 6 cloves garlic, minced
- ¾ cup wine
- 1⅓ cups chicken broth
- ⅔ cup half and half
- ¼ teaspoon ground pepper
- 1 teaspoon salt
- ¼ teaspoon Italian seasoning

Directions:

1. Cook the angel hair pasta according to package instructions. Drain and set aside.
2. To make the chicken, mix the flour, salt, pepper, and Italian seasoning in a bowl. Place the milk in a separate bowl. Lightly pound the chicken tenders, then coat them in flour. Dip into milk and dredge in flour once more.
3. In a large skillet, heat the oil over high heat. Cook each side of the chicken for about 2 minutes. Remove from heat and keep warm.
4. To make the vegetables and sauce, heat the oil in the skillet. Add the peppers and red onion. Sauté for 2 minutes over medium-high heat, stirring occasionally.
5. Add the butter and minced garlic to the vegetables. Sauté for 1 more minute. Add the wine and broth. Reduce heat to medium-low. Let cook for 5 minutes. Add half and half, salt, pepper, and Italian seasoning. Let cook for 1 minute. Add the chicken and pasta. Toss together to blend well. Simmer to warm, then serve.

Nutrition:
489 Calories, 6.8g Carbs, 31g Protein

My notes:

Pub Mac N Cheese Entree

Preparation Time: 20 minutes

Cooking Time: 30 minutes

Servings: 4

Ingredients:

- 8 ounces dry pasta
- 2 tablespoon flour
- 4 tablespoon butter
- 6 ounces beer (we used an IPA)
- 1 tablespoon coarse-ground mustard
- ¼ cup milk
- 6 ounces sharp cheddar cheese, shredded
- 1 cup soft pretzel, diced into ¼" pieces
- 3 ounces Monterey jack cheese, shredded

Directions:

1. Boil the pasta per the Directions mentioned on the package Drain & set aside Now, over moderate heat in a large saucepan; heat 2 tablespoons of butter & mix in 2 tablespoons of flour; cook for a minute or two.
2. Add beer; give the ingredients a good stir until combined well. Add milk & cook until thickened slightly for 5 minutes, stirring frequently. Add mustard & cheese; decreases the heat to low.
3. Now, over moderate heat in a separate pan; heat 2 tablespoons of butter & add in the chopped pretzels, stir to coat nicely with the

butter. Combine pasta with cheese sauce; transfer to an oven safe container & bake for 15 minutes at 350 F.

4. Remove from the oven & sprinkle with pretzel pieces; place into the oven again & bake for 15 minutes more. Serve hot & enjoy.

Nutrition:

894 Calories, 55g Fats, 37g Protein

My notes:

Recipes for Bread

Black and Blue Burger

Preparation Time: 10 minutes
Cooking Time: 55 minutes
Servings: 4

Ingredients:
For Black & Blue Burger:
- 2 pounds ground beef (premium chuck 80/20 blend)
- 1 kosher dill pickle, finely sliced
- 4 soft brioche buns, cut in half
- ¼ head iceberg lettuce, finely sliced
- 12 ounces blue cheese, such as Point Reyes
- 1 heirloom tomato, finely sliced
- ½ Vidalia onion, very finely sliced
- 8 slices applewood smoked bacon, cooked crispy
- ¼ cup canola oil

For Blackening Spice:
- 1 teaspoon cayenne
- 1 tablespoon fresh ground black pepper
- 2 teaspoons ground cumin
- 1 teaspoon paprika
- 2 teaspoons granulated onion
- 1 teaspoon Italian seasoning
- ½ teaspoon chili powder
- 1 teaspoon granulated garlic
- ½ teaspoon kosher salt

For Donkey Sauce:

- 1 cup mayonnaise
- 4 dashes of Worcestershire sauce
- 1 teaspoon yellow mustard
- ¼ cup roasted garlic, minced
- 4 pinches fresh ground black pepper
- ¼ teaspoon kosher salt

For Garlic Butter:

- 4 tablespoons unsalted butter (½ stick)
- 3 tablespoons fresh flat-leaf parsley, minced
- 6 garlic cloves, minced

Directions:

1. For the blackening spice: Combine pepper together with cayenne, granulated onion, cumin, Italian seasoning, granulated garlic, chili powder, paprika & salt in a small-sized mixing bowl. Mix until blended well.

2. For the garlic butter: Over medium heat in a medium saucepan; heat the butter until melted. Add and cook the garlic for 5 to 6 minutes until fragrant. Stir in the parsley. Set aside.

3. For donkey sauce: Combine the roasted garlic together with mayonnaise, mustard, Worcestershire, pepper, and salt in a small mixing bowl; mix well. Cover & reserve. For the black & blue burger: Preheat a grill over medium-high heat.

4. Evenly divide the ground beef into eight portions; roll each into a loose ball, then flatten into a 4" patty. Place 2 ounces of the blue cheese on four of the patties. Cover with a second patty & gently seal the edges to form a stuffed patty approximately 1 ½" thick.

5. Season both sides of the stuffed patties with the blackening spice. Grill for a couple of minutes until a crust has developed on the first side, spread approximately 3" apart. Carefully flip & continue to cook the other side for 2 minutes. Put each burger with 2 slices of bacon & 1 ounce of the leftover blue cheese. Cover with a piece of foil & cook until the cheese is completely melted, for 30 more seconds. Remove the burgers to a serving tray & let rest.

6. Glaze the sides of the brioche buns lightly with garlic butter & toast on the grill for a few seconds, until crisp & golden.

In assembling:

7. Coat the buns with some donkey sauce. Place the bottom buns with a burger, pickles, and onions, then layer it. Top with lettuce and tomatoes. Cover with the bun tops & secure with wooden skewers. Serve immediately & enjoy.

Nutrition:

910 Calories, 61. 3g Fats, 42.6g Protein

My notes:

The Madlove Burger

Preparation Time: 25 minutes
Cooking Time: 1 hour and 20 minutes
Servings: 6

Ingredients:
For the Maple Bacon:

- 12 slices bacon
- ⅓ cup light brown sugar, packed
- ¼ cup pure maple syrup

For the Candied Jalapenos:

- 2 large jalapeno peppers, sliced into rounds
- ¼ cup distilled white vinegar
- ⅓ cup granulated sugar

For the Burgers:

- 12 ounces ground beef chuck
- 6 ounces ground beef brisket
- ⅓ cup seltzer
- 6 ounces ground beef sirloin
- A pinch of Cajun seasoning
- 6 slices provolone cheese
- Unsalted butter, for spreading
- 6 slices mozzarella cheese
- Butter lettuce, sliced tomatoes, and sliced avocado, for topping
- 6 sesame brioche buns, split
- Freshly ground pepper & kosher salt to taste
- 6 slices Swiss cheese
- Vegetable oil, for the grill

Directions:

For Maple Bacon:

1. Preheat your oven to 275 F. Arrange the bacon on a rack set on a rimmed baking sheet & bake in the preheated oven for 30 minutes; brush with some maple syrup & sprinkle with the brown sugar.

Continue to bake until the sugar melts & the bacon is glazed. Let cool.

For Candied Jalapenos:

2. Combine jalapenos together with vinegar and granulated sugar in a small bowl; set aside.

For Burgers:

3. Preheat a grill pan or grill over high heat & brush the grates with the vegetable oil. Combine beef chuck together with brisket and sirloin, Cajun seasoning, seltzer & a pinch each of pepper and salt in a large bowl. Using your hands; mix until just combined. Make six patties, approximately ½" thick from the mixture.

4. Grill the burgers for 3 ½ minutes; flip & top each with a slice of Swiss cheese, provolone, and mozzarella. Cover & cook for 2 ½ minutes more. In the meantime, butter the cut sides of the buns & grill for a minute, until warm.

5. Serve and garnish with the candied jalapenos, maple bacon, lettuce, avocado, and tomato.

Nutrition:

887 Calories0, 59g Fats, 43g Protein

My notes:

A.I. Peppercorn Burger

Preparation Time: 15 minutes
Cooking Time: 20 minutes
Servings: 4

Ingredients:
- Hamburger meat
- Onions
- Montreal steal seasoning
- Onion buns
- Garlic powder
- A1 peppercorn steak sauce
- Ketchup
- Mayonnaise
- Tomatoes
- Pepper jack cheese
- Bacon
- 1 large Egg
- Beer
- Pepper & salt to taste

Directions:
1. Season the hamburger meat with pepper and salt to taste; mix well or just use Red Robin's seasoning salt. Press into the shape of patties. Season the bottom and top of each patty with the garlic powder and Montreal steak seasoning.
2. Let sit at room temperature for 30 to 60 minutes. Combine ⅔ mayo with ⅓ ketchup. Add A1 peppercorn sauce to taste. Grill the burgers until you get your desired doneness.
3. Cut the onions into fine rings and then cut the tomatoes into slices. Combine 1 cup of all-purpose flour together with ½ teaspoon ground black pepper, 1 teaspoon garlic powder, 1 beaten egg & 1 ½ cups of beer; mix well. Dip the onions into the prepared beer batter.

4. Fry the batter covered onions for a couple of minutes, until turn golden brown, and then cook the bacon. Toast the onion buns. Add pepper jack cheese to the patties & let the heat from the grill until the cheese is completely melted.
5. Put a generous amount of peppercorn and brush on both slices of the bun. Load the burger patty, onion straws, bacon & tomato. Serve immediately & enjoy.

Nutrition:
908 Calories, 62g Fats, 43g Protein

My notes:

Chili's 1975 Soft Tacos

Preparation Time: 20 minutes

Cooking Time: 12 hours and 15 minutes

Servings: 6

Ingredients:

- 1 ½ pounds beef chuck pot roast, fat trimmed
- 12 corn tortillas (6" each)
- 5 teaspoons chili powder
- 2 jars mild or medium tomato-based salsa (16 ounces each)
- 3 cups fresh lettuce, shredded
- 1 avocado
- 2 tablespoons cider vinegar
- ¾ cup sour cream

Directions:

1. Spoon a cup of salsa into a small bowl & reserve. Combine the leftover salsa with chili powder and vinegar in a slow cooker. Add beef; cover & cook for 10 to 12 hours on low-heat, until the beef shreds easily. Shred the meat, using two forks & spoon into a large-sized serving bowl.

2. Preheat oven to 300 F. Stack the tortillas, wrap in foil & bake in the preheated oven for 8 to 10 minutes, until warm. Place lettuce and sour cream in bowls. Just before serving; pit, peel & dice the avocado & place in a small bowl.

Put out the bowls (including the salsa) & assemble tacos at the table.

Nutrition:
901 Calories, 62g Fats, 42g Protein

My notes:

Sweet and Savory Snack Recipes

Chocolate Wave

Preparation Time: 25 minutes

Cooking Time: 5 hours 15 minutes

Servings: 6

Ingredients:
- 4 organic eggs, large
- 1 cup sugar
- 2 ½ teaspoons cornstarch
- ¾ cup butter
- 4 egg yolks
- 1 cup semisweet chocolate chips
- 1 ½ teaspoon Grand Marnier

For White-Chocolate Truffle:
- 3 tablespoons heavy cream
- 6 ounces white chocolate
- 2 tablespoons Grand Marnier
- 3 tablespoons softened butter

Directions:
1. Over medium-low heat in a double boiler; melt the butter. Add in the chocolate chips; continue to heat until the mixture is completely melted.
2. Combine cornstarch and sugar in a large-sized mixing bowl. Add the chocolate mixture into the sugar mixture; beat well.
3. Combine four yolks with four eggs & Grand Marnier in a separate bowl. Add this to the chocolate mixture; continue to beat until mixed well. Cover & let chill for overnight.

For Truffle:
4. Over low heat in a double boiler; melt the white chocolate with heavy cream. Add Grand Marnier and butter; give the ingredients a good stir until completely smooth. Chill for overnight.
5. Lightly coat 5-ounce ramekins with butter & then dust with flour, filling approximately 1/3 of the chilled chocolate mixture. Add a

rounded tablespoon of the truffle mixture. Fill to the top with the chocolate mixture.

6. Bake for 15 minutes at 450 F. Let the cakes to sit for 15 to 20 minutes before inverting. Run a knife around the edges to loosen. Serve with raspberries, chocolate sauce, and/or ice cream.

Nutrition:

302 Calories, 22g Fats, 28g Carbs, 35g Protein

My notes:

Houston's Apple Walnut Cobbler

Preparation Time: 15 minutes

Cooking Time: 30 minutes

Servings: 6

My notes:

Ingredients:

- 3 large Granny Smith apples, peeled and diced
- 1½ cups walnuts, coarsely chopped
- 1 cup all-purpose flour
- 1 cup brown sugar
- 1 teaspoon cinnamon
- Pinch of nutmeg
- 1 large egg
- ½ cup (1 stick) butter, melted
- Vanilla ice cream
- Caramel sauce, for drizzling

Directions:

1. Preheat oven to 350°F. Lightly grease an 8-inch square baking dish. Spread diced apple over the bottom of the baking dish.
2. Sprinkle with walnuts. In a bowl, mix together flour, sugar, cinnamon, nutmeg, and egg to make a coarse-textured mixture.
3. Sprinkle over the apple-walnut layer. Pour melted butter over the whole mixture. Bake until fragrant and crumb top is browned (about 30 minutes). Serve warm topped with scoops of vanilla ice cream.
4. Drizzle with caramel sauce.

Nutrition:

611 Calories, 36g Fats, 69g Carbs, 8g Protein

Papa John's Cinnapie

Preparation Time: 5 minutes
Cooking Time: 12 minutes
Servings: 12

My notes:

Ingredients:

- 1 whole pizza dough
- 1 tablespoon melted butter
- 2 tablespoons cinnamon,
  or to taste

Topping

- ¾ cup flour
- ½ cup white sugar
- 1/3 cup brown sugar
- 2 tablespoons oil
- 2 tablespoons shortening

Icing:

- 1½ cups powdered sugar
- 3 tablespoons milk
- ¾ teaspoon vanilla

Directions:

1. Preheat oven to 460°F. Grease or spray a pizza pan or baking sheet.
2. Brush the dough evenly with melted butter. Sprinkle with cinnamon. Place the ingredients for the topping in a bowl and toss together with a fork.
3. Sprinkle topping over the dough. Bake until fragrant and lightly browned at the edges (about 10–12 minutes). Mix the icing ingredients together in a bowl. If too thick, gradually add in a little more milk. Drizzle icing over warm pizza.

Nutrition:

560 Calories, 90g Carbs, 19g Fats, 8g Protein

Chipotle's Refried Beans

Preparation Time: 5 minutes
Cooking Time: 5 minutes
Servings: 6

Ingredients:

- 1-pound dried pinto beans
- 6 cups warm water
- ½ cup bacon fat
- 2 teaspoons salt
- 1 teaspoon cumin
- ½ teaspoon black pepper
- ½ teaspoon cayenne pepper

Directions:

1. Rinse and drain the pinto beans. Check them over and remove any stones. Place the beans in a Dutch oven and add the water. Bring the pot to a boil, reduce the heat, and simmer for 2 hours, stirring frequently.
2. When the beans are tender, reserve ½ cup of the boiling water and drain the rest. Heat the bacon fat in a large, deep skillet. Add the beans 1 cup at a time, mashing and stirring as you go. Add the spices and some of the cooking liquid if the beans are too dry.

Nutrition:

100 Calories, 18g Carbs, 1g Fats, 6g Protein

Cracker Barrel Fried Apples

Preparation Time: 10 minutes
Cooking Time: 20 minutes
Servings: 8

Ingredients:

- 6 Tart apples
- ¼ cup, or butter Bacon drippings
- 4 tablespoons Lemon juice
- 1/8 teaspoon Salt
- ¼ cup Brown sugar
- 1 pinch Ground nutmeg
- 1 tsp Ground cinnamon

Directions:

1. Melt the butter or bacon drippings in a large skillet. Evenly spread the apples at the bottom of the skillet. Sprinkle the lemon juice on top, followed by salt and brown sugar.
2. Cover with the lid and cook over low heat for about fifteen minutes, or until the apples are juicy and tender. Sprinkle the nutmeg and cinnamon on top and serve. You may add a squeeze of lemon on top if desired.
3. Take a medium saucepan, place it over low heat, add butter and erythritol and then cook for 4 to 5 minutes until butter melts and turns golden brown.

4. Stir in cream, bring it to a gentle boil and then simmer the sauce for 10 minutes until the sauce has thickened to coat the back of the spoon, stirring constantly.
5. Remove pan from heat, stir in vanilla extract and then serve.

Nutrition:

78 Calories, 15mg Cholesterol, 7g Carbs

My notes:

Dessert & Pastry Recipes

NUT BROWNIES

MAKES 16 BROWNIES

MEAS. AND SIFT TOGETHER.
1 CUP SIFTED FLOUR
1 TEASPOON BAKING POWDE.
5 TABLESPOONS COCOA
WORK WITH SPOON UNTIL SOFT.
1/2 CUP SHORTENING
1/2 CUP SUGAR
BEAT UNTIL LIGHT AND FLUFFY.
THEN ADD: 1 EGG -1TEASP. VANI
LLA. BEAT UNTIL WELL BLENDED
ADD.1/2 CUP DARK CORN SYRUP
  GRADUALLY ADD SIFTED DRY
  INGREDIENTS. AND ADD 1/2
  CUP BROKEN WALNUTS MIX WELL
  SPREAD MIXTURE INTO A
  GREASED SQUARE PAN. BAKE IN A
  SLOW OVEN(325F.) 30 MINUTES.
COOL-CUT IN SQUARES, STORE
IN BREAD BOX.

Cherry Chocolate Cobbler

Preparation Time: 10 minutes
Cooking Time: 45 minutes
Servings: 8

Ingredients:

- 1½ cups all-purpose flour
- ½ cup sugar
- 2 teaspoons baking powder
- ½ teaspoon salt
- ¼ cup butter
- 6 ounces semisweet chocolate morsels
- ¼ cup milk
- 1 egg, beaten
- 21 ounces cherry pie filling
- ½ cup finely chopped nuts

Directions:

1. Preheat the oven to 350°F. Combine the flour, sugar, baking powder, salt, and butter in a large mixing bowl. Use a pastry blender to cut the mixture until there are lumps the size of small peas.
2. Melt the chocolate morsels. Let cool for approximately 5 minutes, then add the milk and egg and mix well. Beat into the flour mixture, mixing completely. Spread the pie filling in a 2-quart casserole dish. Randomly drop the chocolate batter over the filling, then sprinkle with nuts.
3. Bake for 40–45 minutes. Serve with a scoop of vanilla ice cream if desired.

Nutrition:

45g Carbs, 14g Fats, 3g Protein

Pumpkin Custard with Gingersnaps

Preparation Time: 30 minutes

Cooking Time 35 minutes

Servings: 8

Ingredients:
- Custard
- 8 egg yolks
- 1¾ cups (1 15-ounce can) pure pumpkin puree
- 1¾ cups heavy whipping cream
- ½ cup sugar
- 1½ teaspoons pumpkin pie spice
- 1 teaspoon vanilla

Topping:
- 1 cup crushed gingersnap cookies
- 1 tablespoon melted butter

Whipped Cream:
- 1 cup heavy whipping cream
- 1 tablespoon superfine sugar (or regular sugar if you have no caster sugar)
- ½ teaspoon pumpkin pie spice

Garnish:
- 8 whole gingersnap cookies

Directions:
1. Preheat the oven to 350°F. Separate the yolks from 8 eggs and whisk them together in a large mixing bowl until they are well blended and creamy.
2. Add the pumpkin, sugar, vanilla, heavy cream, and pumpkin pie spice and whisk to combine. Cook the custard mixture in a double boiler, stirring until it has thickened enough that it coats a spoon.
3. Pour the mixture into individual custard cups or an 8×8-inch baking pan and bake for about 20 minutes if using individual cups or 30–35

minutes for the baking pan, until it is set and a knife inserted comes out clean.

4. While the custard is baking, make the topping by combining the crushed gingersnaps and melted butter. After the custard has been in the oven for 15 minutes, sprinkle the gingersnap mixture over the top.

5. When the custard has passed the clean knife test, remove from the oven, and let cool to room temperature. Whisk the heavy cream and pumpkin pie spice together with the caster sugar and beat just until it thickens. Serve the custard with the whipped cream and garnish each serving with a gingersnap.

Nutrition:

44g Carbs, 14g Fats, 3g Protein

My notes:

Baked Apple Dumplings

Preparation Time: 20 minutes

Cooking Time 40 minutes

Servings: 2–4

Ingredients:

- 1 (17½ ounce) package frozen puff pastry, thawed
- 1 cup sugar
- 6 tablespoons dry breadcrumbs
- 2 teaspoons ground cinnamon
- 1 pinch ground nutmeg
- 1 egg, beaten
- 4 Granny Smith apples, peeled, cored, and halved
- Vanilla ice cream for serving

Icing:

- 1 cup confectioners' sugar
- 1 teaspoon vanilla extract
- 3 tablespoons milk

Pecan Streusel:

- ⅔ cup chopped toasted pecans
- ⅔ cup packed brown sugar
- ⅔ cup all-purpose flour
- 5 tablespoons melted butter

Directions:

1. Preheat the oven to 425°F. When the puff pastry has completely thawed, roll out each sheet to measure 12 inches by 12 inches. Cut the sheets into quarters. Combine the sugar, breadcrumbs, cinnamon, and nutmeg together in a small bowl.
2. Brush one of the pastry squares with some of the beaten egg. Add about 1 tablespoon of the breadcrumb mixture on top, then add half an apple, core side down, over the crumbs. Add another tablespoon of the breadcrumb mixture.

3. Seal the dumpling by pulling up the corners and pinching the pastry together until the seams are totally sealed. Repeat this process with the remaining squares. Assemble the ingredients for the pecan streusel in a small bowl.

4. Grease a baking sheet or line it with parchment paper. Place the dumplings on the sheet and brush them with a bit more of the beaten egg. Top with the pecan streusel.

5. Bake for 15 minutes, then reduce heat to 350°F and bake for 25 minutes more or until lightly browned. Make the icing by combining the confectioners' sugar, vanilla, and milk until you reach the proper consistency.

6. When the dumplings are done, let them cool to room temperature and drizzle them with icing before serving.

Nutrition:

43g Carbs, 13g Fats, 3.1g Protein

My notes:

Peach Cobbler

Preparation Time: 10 minutes
Cooking Time 45 minutes
Servings: 4

Ingredients:
- 1¼ cups Bisquick
- 1 cup milk
- ½ cup melted butter
- ¼ teaspoon nutmeg
- ½ teaspoon cinnamon
- Vanilla ice cream, for serving

Filling:
- 1 (30-ounce) can peaches in syrup, drained
- ¼ cup sugar

Topping:
- ½ cup brown sugar
- ¼ cup almond slices
- ½ teaspoon cinnamon
- 1 tablespoon melted butter

Directions:
1. Preheat the oven to 375°F. Grease the bottom and sides of an 8×8-inch pan. Whisk together the Bisquick, milk, butter, nutmeg, and cinnamon in a large mixing bowl. When thoroughly combined, pour into the greased baking pan.

2. Mix together the peaches and sugar in another mixing bowl. Put the filling on top of the batter in the pan. Bake for about 45 minutes.

3. In another bowl, mix together the brown sugar, almonds, cinnamon, and melted butter. After the cobbler has cooked for 45 minutes, cover evenly with the topping and bake for an additional 10 minutes. Serve with a scoop of vanilla ice cream.

Nutrition:

41g Carbs, 13g Fats, 4g Protein

My notes:

Homemade Walnut Cherry Brownies

Preparation Time: 20 minutes

Cooking Time 25-30 minutes

Servings: 6-9

Ingredients:

- 9 fresh cherries that are stemmed and pitted or 9 frozen cherries
- ½ teaspoon cornstarch
- ¼ teaspoon cinnamon
- Dash ground nutmeg
- ¼ cup brown sugar
- ¼ cup applesauce
- ¼ teaspoon vanilla extract
- 1 tablespoon butter, melted
- 1 sheet of puff pastry, thawed
- Whipped cream or vanilla ice cream, to serve

Directions:

1. Turn on the oven temperature to 375 degrees F. and grease a 9-inch square baking pan.
2. Take a large bowl and add the oil and sugar or sweetener substitute and mix the ingredients well, adding the eggs.
3. Pour in the yogurt and continue to mix the mixture until smooth.
4. Take a medium bowl and combine the cocoa powder, flour, sea salt, and baking powder by mixing them.
5. Combine the powdered ingredients with the wet ingredients and use your electronic mixer to incorporate the ingredients well.
6. Add the walnuts and mix.
7. Pour the mixture into the pan.
8. Sprinkle the cherries on top and push them into the batter. You can use any design, but it's best to make three rows and three columns with the cherries. This ensures that each piece of the brownie will have a cherry.

9. Place the batter in the oven and set the timer to 20 minutes.
10. Check that the brownies are done using the toothpick test before removing them from the oven. Push the toothpick into the middle of the brownies and when it comes out clean, remove the brownies.
11. Allow the brownies to cool for 5-10 minutes before cutting and serving.

Nutrition:

225 Calories, 10g Fats, 5g Protein

My notes:

Blackout Cake

My notes:

Preparation Time: 30 minutes
Cooking Time: 35–45 minutes
Servings: 8 - 10

Ingredients:
For the Cake:
- 1 cup butter, softened
- 4 cups sugar
- 4 large eggs
- 4 teaspoons vanilla extract, divided
- 6 ounces unsweetened chocolate, melted
- 4 cups flour
- 4 teaspoons baking soda
- ½ teaspoon salt
- 1 cup buttermilk
- 1 ¾ cups boiling water

For the Chocolate Ganache:
- 12 ounces semisweet chocolate, chips or chopped
- 3 cups heavy cream
- 4 tablespoons butter, chopped
- 2 teaspoons vanilla
- 1 ½ cups roasted almonds, crushed (for garnish)

Directions:
1. Preheat the oven to 350°F. Prepare two large rimmed baking sheets with parchment paper (or grease and dust with flour 3 8-inch cake pans).
2. In a large bowl or bowl for a stand mixer, beat together the butter and sugar until well combined. When the sugar mixture is fluffy, add the eggs and 2 teaspoons of vanilla. When that is combined, add the 4 ounces of melted chocolate and mix well.
3. In a separate bowl, stir together the flour, baking soda, and salt. Gradually add half the flour mixture to the chocolate mixture. When

it is combined, add half of the buttermilk and mix until combined. Repeat with remaining flour mixture and buttermilk. When it is completely combined, add the boiling water and mix thoroughly. (The batter should be a little thin).

4. Divide the batter evenly between the two large baking sheets that you prepared earlier (or 3 8-inch cake pans).

5. Transfer to the oven and bake for 20–30 minutes for the baking sheets or 25-35 minutes for the cake pans, or until a toothpick inserted in the center comes out clean.

6. Remove from the oven and let cakes cool for about 10 minutes. With the pastry ring, make 3 cakes from each of the baking sheets. When they are completely cool down. If using cake pans, turn them out onto a cooling rack and let them cool completely and then cut horizontally into two to make 6 cake layers.

7. Make the ganache by mixing the chocolate chips and cream in a heat-safe glass bowl. Place the bowl over a pot of boiling water. Reduce heat to medium-low and let simmer gently. Stir constantly with a wooden spoon until the chocolate is all melted. Add-in the butter and vanilla and stir until well combined. Let cool for a few minutes, cover with plastic wrap, and refrigerate until the ganache holds its shape and is spreadable, about 10 minutes.

8. To assemble the cake, place the first cake layer on a serving plate and spread some of the ganache on the top. Place the second cake layer on top and spread some of the ganache on top. Repeat until all 6 layers are done. Use the remaining ganache to frost the top and sides of the cake, then cover the sides with crushed almonds (if desired) by pressing them gently into the chocolate ganache. Refrigerate before serving.

Nutrition:
41g Carbs, 10g Fats, 4g Protein

Molten Lava Cake

Preparation Time: 20 minutes
Cooking Time: 10 minutes
Servings: 5-6

Ingredients:
For the Cakes:

- Six tablespoons unsalted butter (2 tablespoons melted, four tablespoons at room temperature)
- 1/2 cup natural cocoa powder (not Dutch process), plus more for dusting
- 1 1/3 cups all-purpose flour
- One teaspoon baking soda
- 1/2 teaspoon baking powder
- 1/2 teaspoon salt
- Three tablespoons milk
- 1/4 cup vegetable oil
- 1 1/3 cups sugar
- 1 1/2 teaspoons vanilla extract
- Two large eggs, at room temperature

For the Fillings and Toppings:

- 8 ounces bittersweet chocolate, finely chopped
- 1/2 cup heavy cream
- Four tablespoons unsalted butter
- One tablespoon light corn syrup
- Caramel sauce, for drizzling

- 1-pint vanilla ice cream

Directions:

1. Oven preheats to 350 degrees F. Make the cakes: Brush four one 1/4-cup brioche molds (jumbo muffin cups or 10-ounce ramekins) with the butter melted in 2 tablespoons. Clean the cocoa powdered molds and tap the excess.

2. In a small bowl, whisk in the flour, baking soda, baking powder, and salt. Bring 3/4 cup water& the milk and over medium heat to a boil in a saucepan; set aside.

3. Use a stand mixer, combine vegetable oil, four tablespoons of room-temperature butter and sugar and beat with the paddle attachment until it's fluffy at medium-high speed, around 4 minutes, scrape the bowl down and beat as desired. Add 1/2 cup cocoa powder and vanilla; beat over medium velocity for 1 minute. Scrape the pot beneath. Add one egg and beat at medium-low speed for 1 minute, then add the remaining egg and beat for another minute.

4. Gradually beat in the flour mixture with the mixer on a low level, then the hot milk mixture. Finish combining the batter with a spatula of rubber before mixed. Divide the dough equally between the molds, each filling slightly more than three-quarters of the way.

5. Move the molds to a baking sheet and bake for 25 to 30 minutes, until the tops of the cakes feel domed, and the centers are just barely set. Move the baking sheet to a rack; allow the cakes to cool for about 30 minutes before they pull away from the molds.

6. How to set up the Cake: Make the Filling: Microwave the sugar, butter, chocolate, and corn syrup in a microwave-safe bowl at intervals of 30 seconds, stirring each time, until the chocolate starts to melt, 1 minute, 30 seconds. Let sit for three minutes and then whisk until smooth. Reheat, if possible, before use.

7. Using a paring knife tip to remove the cakes gently from the molds, then invert the cakes onto a cutting board.

8. Hollow out a spoon to the cake; save the scraps. Wrap the plastic wrap and microwave cakes until steaming, for 1 minute.

9. Drizzle the caramel plates, unwrap the cakes, then put them on top. Pour three tablespoons into each cake filling.
10. Plug in a cake scrap to the door. Save any leftover scraps or discard them.
11. Top each cake, use an ice cream scoop. Spoon more chocolate sauce on top, spread thinly so that it is coated in a jar.

Nutrition:

546 Calories, 5g Protein, 61g Carbohydrate, 31g Fats

My notes:

White Chocolate Raspberry Nothing Bundt Cakes

Preparation Time: 20 minutes

Cooking Time: 10 minutes

Servings: 5-6

Ingredients:

- Chopped into small cubes, 200g butter, plus extra for greasing
- 100g white chocolate, broken into pieces
- Four large eggs
- 200g caster sugar
- 200g self-rising flour
- 175g raspberries, fresh or frozen

For the ganache:

- 200g white chocolate, chopped
- 250ml double cream
- A little icing sugar, for dusting

Directions:

1. Heat oven to fan/gas 4, 180C/160C. Grease and line the 2 x 20 cm round base with loose-bottomed cake tins. In a heat-proof mixing bowl, place the butter and chocolate, set over a pan of barely simmering water, and allow to melt gradually, stirring occasionally.
2. Once butter and chocolate have melted, remove from heat and cool for 1-2 minutes, then beat with an electric whisk in the eggs and sugar. Fold and raspberries in the starch.

3. Pour the mixture gently into the tins and bake for 20-25 minutes or until golden brown and a skewer inserted in the center is clean (Don't be fooled by their juiciness, the raspberries leave a residue on the skewer). Pullout the cakes from the oven & allow for 10 minutes of cooling in the tins before placing on a wire rack.

4. To make the ganache, place the chocolate over a pan of barely simmering water in a heatproof bowl with 100ml of the cream on top. Remove until the chocolate has melted into the sugar, and leave a smooth, shiny ganache on you. You need to leave the ganache at room temperature to cool, then beat in the rest of the cream.

5. Sandwich them together with the chocolate ganache after the cakes have cooled. Just before serving, sprinkle them with icing sugar.

Nutrition:

489 Calories, 3.9g Protein, 59g Carbohydrate, 28g Fats

My notes:

Caramel Rockslide Brownies

Preparation Time: 25 minutes

Cooking Time: 25 minutes

Servings: 5-6

Ingredients:
- 1 cup butter (2 sticks)
- 2 cups of sugar
- Four eggs
- Two teaspoons vanilla extract
- 2/3 cup unsweetened natural cocoa powder
- 1 cup all-purpose flour
- 1/2 teaspoon salt
- One teaspoon baking powder
- 1/2 cup semisweet chocolate chips
- 1 cup (plus more for drizzling over the top) caramel topping
- 3/4 cup chopped pecans (plus more for sprinkling on top)

Directions:
1. Preheat to 350 degrees on the oven. On a medium saucepan, melt butter over medium heat.
2. Clear from heat the pan and whisk in sugar. Whisk in the vanilla extract & the eggs. Mix the cocoa, baking powder, flour, salt and in a separate dish. Drop the dry ingredients into the saucepan and combine them until they have just been added. Add chocolate chips.
3. Pour the batter into two nine by 9-inch baking pans that are evenly split, sprayed with nonstick spray, and lined with parchment paper.
4. Bake for 25-28 minutes and leave to cool.
5. Use the parchment paper edges to lift the whole brownie out of one of the pans, and chop into 1/2-inch cubes.
6. Pour 1 cup of caramel over the brownies still in the saucepan, then add the chopped pecans and brownie cubes.

7. Press down to make the caramel stick to the brownie cubes. If desired, drizzle with extra caramel and sprinkle with a few more chopped pecans.
8. If needed, serve with ice cream and excess sugar, and chopped pecans.

Nutrition:

509 Calories, 5g Protein, 67g Carbohydrate, 32g Fats

My notes:

Delicious Ideas for Kids

Have you ever had the experience that you cooked for a long time and then your child did not want to eat?
Even their big guests are happy about lovingly prepared dishes.

Here are some suggestions:

Practical Advice for Beginners to Canning and Preserving your favorite Foods

There are a few safety tips that you should follow when you start canning and preserving foods from home. Canning is a great way to store and preserve foods, but it can be risky if not done correctly. However, if you follow these tips, you will be able to can foods safely.

Choose the Right Canner

The first step to safe home canning is choosing the right canner. First off, know when to use a pressure canner or a water bath canner.

Use a pressure canner that is specifically designed for canning and preserving foods. There are several types of canner out there, and some are just for cooking food, not for preserving food and processing jars. Be sure that you have the right type of equipment.

Make sure your pressure canner is the right size. If your canner is too small, the jars may be undercooked. Always opt for a larger canner as the pressure on the bigger pots tends to be more accurate, and you will be able to take advantage of the larger size and can more foods at once!

Before you begin canning, check that your pressure canner is in good condition. If your canner has a rubber gasket, it should be flexible and soft. If the rubber is dry or cracked, it should be replaced before you start canning. Be sure your canner is clean, and the small vents in the lid are free of debris. Adjust your canner for high altitude processing if needed.

Once you are sure your canner is ready to go and meets all these guidelines, it is time to start canning!

Opt for a Screw Top Lid System

There are many kinds of canning jars that you can choose to purchase. However, the only type of jar approved by the USDA is a mason jar with a screw-top lid. These are designated "preserving jars" and are considered the safest and most effective option for home preserving uses.

Some jars are not thought to be safe for home preservation despite being marketed as canning jars. Bail Jars, for example, have a two-part wire clasp lid with a rubber ring in between the lid and jar. While these were popular in the past, it is now thought that the thick rubber and tightly closed lid does not provide a sufficient seal, leading to a higher potential for botulism. Lightening Jars should not be used for canning as they are simply glass jars with glass lids, with no rubber at all. That will not create a good seal!

Reusing jars from store-bought products is another poor idea. They may look like they're in good condition, but they are typically designed to be processed in a commercial facility. Most store-bought products do not have the two-part band and lid system, which is best for home canning. The rubber seal on a store-bought product is likely not reusable once you open the original jar. You can reuse store-bought jars at home for storage but not for canning and preserving.

Check Your Jars, Lids, and Bands

As you wash your jars with soapy water, check for any imperfections. Even new jars may have a small chip or crack and need to be discarded. You can reuse jars again and again as long as they are in good condition.
The metal jar rings are also reusable; however, you should only reuse them if they are rust free and undented. If your bands begin to show signs of wear, consider investing in some new ones.

Jar lids need to be new as the sealing compound on the lid can disintegrate over time. When you store your jars in damp places (like in a basement or canning cellar), the lids are even more likely to disintegrate. Always use new lids to ensure that your canning is successful.

Check for Recent Canning Updates

Canning equipment has changed over the years, becoming higher-tech and, therefore, more efficient at processing foods. In addition to the equipment becoming more advanced, there have also been many scientific improvements, making canning safer when the proper steps are taken. For example, many people used to sterilize their jars before pressure canning. While this is still okay to do, it is unnecessary as science has shown that any bacteria in the jars will die when heated to such a high temperature in a pressure canner. Sterilization is an extra step that you don't need!
Make sure that your food preservation information is all up to date and uses current canning guidelines. Avoid outdated cookbooks and reassess "trusted family methods" to make sure they fit into the most recent criteria for safe canning. When in doubt, check with the US Department of Agriculture's Complete Guide to Home Canning, which contains the most recent, up-to-date canning tips.

Pick the Best Ingredients

When choosing food to can, always get the best food possible. You want to use high quality, perfectly ripe produce for canning. You will never end up with a jar of food better than the product itself, so picking good ingredients is important to your final product's taste. Also, products that past their prime can affect the ability to handle it. If strawberries are overripe, your jam may come out too runny. If your tomatoes are past their prime, they may not have a high enough pH level to be processed in a water bath. Pick your ingredients well, and you will make successfully preserved foods.

Clean everything

While you may know that your jars and lids need to be washed and sanitized, don't forget about the rest of your tools. Cleaning out your canner before using it is essential, even if you put it away clean. Make sure to wipe your countertop well, making sure there are no crumbs or residue. Wash your produce with clean, cold water, and don't forget to wash your hands! The cleaner everything is, the less likely you are to spread bacteria onto your jarred foods.

Follow Your Recipe

Use recipes from trusted sources, and be sure to follow them to the letter. Changing the amount of one or two ingredients may alter the balance of acidity and result in unsafe canning (especially when using a water bath canner). Use the ingredients as directed and make very few changes—none if possible.

Adhere to the processing times specified by your recipe. Sometimes the times may seem a little long, but the long processing time makes these products safe to store on the shelf. The processing time is the correct amount of time needed to destroy spoilage organisms, mold spores, yeast, and pathogens in the jar. So, as you may have guessed, it is extremely important to use the times written in your recipe as a hard rule.

Cool the Jars

Be sure that you give your jars 12 hours to cool before testing the seal. If you test the seal too early, it may break as the jar is still warm, making it pliable. Be sure to cool the jars away from a window or fan as even a slight breeze may cause the hot jars to crack. Once cool, remove the metal band, clean it and save it for your next canning project.

Conclusion

Dear Reader,

We're on the last few pages of this book, and I'd like to ask you how much you enjoyed flipping through it.

Did you find any new recipes for your lunch and dinner?

Did you enjoy them on your own or with someone else?

And what did you think of the suggestions in the children's pages?

Maybe you've chosen from the index the recipes you've heard of before or those recipes that remind you of something you've already eaten with family and friends. Maybe you'll want to try all the recipes in this book.

... Take your time.

While you were reading, you probably also noticed how many and what dishes you can combine to surprise your guests, or maybe you found recipes that would taste better by changing a few ingredients and adding your personal touch.

Did you jot down your ideas in the notes section next to the recipes?

Have you noted in the tab below which page your favorite recipes are on?

Whether you're good in the kitchen or not, the recipes in this book are easy to prepare, don't require too many ingredients, and will allow you to recreate new masterworks every day that you, your family, and your guests will love.

A reason I sought out so-called "secret recipes" is the fact that once I found my favorite ones, I could enjoy them and combine them whenever I wanted to in the comfort of my own home.

Imagine being able to surprise your friends and family each time with the food they
most enjoyed at famous restaurants.

Imagine how satisfying it would be to show them that you created those masterworks in the comfort of your kitchen with these copycat recipes!

If you're in the mood for more tasty, easy-to-prepare recipes, contact your local bookseller and don't miss our upcoming cookbooks.

Also, by William Oliver Thomas & Ernest D.W.:

Copycat Dessert & Pastry Recipes for Beginners:
Discover how you can surprise your family and guests with these 50 easy, tasty, and low-cost recipes.

Copycat Recipes Beginner's guide:
Discover how you easily prepare delicious snacks, fresh fruit salads, and quenching soft drinks in a short time.

Copycat Cooking for Beginners:
How to leave your family and friends speechless by recreating these famous restaurant recipes.

Beginners Guide to cooking Copycat Dishes:
How to satisfy with pleasure your five senses by preparing quickly and simply these 50 recipes.

Where are your sweetheart recipes?

Title   **Page**

_____

_____

_____

_____

_____

_____

_____

_____

_____

_____

_____

_____

_____

_____

_____

_____

_____

_____

_____

_____

_____

_____

_____

_____

_____

CPSIA information can be obtained
at www.ICGtesting.com
Printed in the USA
BVHW090004020621
608546BV00007B/1066